POEMS

THE THREE HARES
& OTHER MEMORIES

AARON ERICKSEN

JALAPEÑO PUBLISHING
COLLEGE PARK, MARYLAND

Published by Jalapeño Publishing
www.jalapenopublishing.com
Copyright © 2016 Aaron Ericksen
All rights reserved
Manufactured in the United States of America

An Jalapeño Publishing Original
FIRST PRINTING

Editor: Brittany Micka-Foos
Cover Art: Akiko Kobayashi
Artwork: Ellie Maloney
Typeface: Libre Baskerville, Lato, Aquilline II

LIBRARY OF CONGRESS CATALOGING IN PUBLICATION DATA
Ericksen, Aaron 1957–
    The three hares & other memories: poems / Aaron Ericksen
    ISBN 978-0-9983614-0-6

For Lenore and Silas

Acknowledgements

The author wishes to thank his family for their love and support. A very special thanks to Oksana Sudoma; without your love and unwavering support this book would not have happened.

The author also thanks the editors of Scaffolding Magazine in which the following poem appeared: On the Road with Jack Kerouac.

Finally, the author wishes to acknowledge the invaluable contribution s of three courageous Ukrainian poets Taras Shevchenko, Mikhail Bulgakov, and David Vogel. Without their work this book would not exist.

Contents

I. The Three Hares
- The First Gate 2
- Dusk 4
- The Second Gate 6
- Dreams & Paradoila 8
- The Book of Remembrance 10
- The Third Gate 12
- Exit the Noumenon 14

II: AI
- Antic Interpretations 18
- Arcane Infallibility 19
- Anno Inventionis 21
- Appreciative Inquiry 23
- Lorem Ipsum 25
- Fantastic Servant, Horrible Master 27
- Ad Infinitum 29
- AI 31

III: Other Memories
- Song to a Dying Post 34
- Extracting Gold 36
- Carnival Dream 38
- *On the Road* with Jack Kerouac 40
- The Waking of a Myth 41
- Surf's Faint Roar 42
- Sparkling Eyes Zwedru 44
- The Quiet One 45
- Sagrada Familia 46
- The Last Word 48
- Coda 49

The Three Hares

*Three hares sharing three ears,
Yet every one of them has two.*

—Ancient German Riddle

I. The First Gate

One autumn night, on crumbling surface
we counted four million holes.
Blackened pits looming, like a silhouette of souls
leached from earth's crusty furnace
no time to count them all—on the road to Sataniv.

Once a post for the conspicuous and colorful
this Pale attracted poet and reader alike.
Amidst barren fields surrounding this shtetl
we found ourselves, not surprisingly in the married life
searching for the Poet born here.

Each disintegrating hole echoed
four centuries drenched in ink.
Khmelnytsky's uprising, Cossacks' pyre,
buried alive, cut to pieces, forced to kill
horrors covered the steppes like dust.

Fertile ground revives the tree of life!
The revival of Hasidism
foretells the return of the Messiah,
the teachings of Lion Ashkenazi,
and the arrival of the Poet King.

Yet murder begets the elders' banning
wedding celebrations,
fire dances, and masquerades.
Frank's followers accused of religious orgies
were sentenced to 400 lashes.

Rescued from Pogroms,
they return only to find their homes looted
and Holodomor on the horizon.
Even comic entertainers
lost their sense of humor in those days.

The Germans captured the town in forty-one.
Several Jews were shot to death then,
while the Gendarmerie locked 200 into a mournful cellar;
women, children, and the old
died by suffocation and starvation.

180 Jews shot near the Old Synagogue.
The final few taken to Yarmolintsy
where they too were shot.
With no one left to celebrate
Sataniv was liberated by the Red Army in forty-four.

II. Dusk

A thin vein of sky
reddened steadily o'er the farmland's carpet
a little white cloud drifted by
turning grey on one side
as we arrived in Sataniv mid-May.

Like a sink upon a dismal desert
empty streets testify
the crumbling chaos of neglect.
Even when amusement parks are abandoned,
they are full of danger!

Now Sataniv of Podillya
like fallen angel Pripyat
forever bids the sun to lower
like a folding curtain
down to where angels slumber unaware.

Long gone the Hasidic Rebbe in exotic attire
no more poor beggar in the shtetl market
so copiously represented in daguerreotype
when the shtetl was just a shtetl
nothing more, nothing less.

We pass a horse-drawn cart
lumbering towards the market stall
nay, one summers eve in May
we pause to inquire
where to find a place to stay.

Pointing first to the right, then left
the kurkul shrugs
directing in restrained voice
as if not to startle the horse
or wake the town's slumbering souls.

Down the open road
strewn with bricks and ruins
we'd find our destiny
as if in a dream, a Masonic comedy
in a vacuous Galician café.

Dusk settled on barren streets—thick air
of despair and sensuality.
Maria our waitress seats us
bearing the dignity of tedium and a faint tattoo—
three hares circling in symmetry.

III. The Second Gate

In the dining room, dim and sparse
embellished ceilings of basilisks reveal
the gypsy fortuneteller, Mykyta of Bucovina,
daughter of Usari, Maria's mother,
descendant of Athingani.

Gazing our way, Mykyta
hums a Romanian tune,
melodious rhythms of loss and gain
early warnings of a ministering wind
transcending space and time.

Fap, fap, fap—tarot cards descend
from fingers worn by wind, and spirit
images side by side
smuggle mythological motifs
into archetypes of transformation.

Fap, fap, fap—Mykyta queried,
    Where have ye come from?
beneath a larger choir of sound, mirrored
through clouds of cognition, inheriting
constellations primordial.

Mystical visions of three poet angels
and three poems buried
puzzle pieces from the seven heavens
legacy etched in stones.
    Is that of which ye seek?

Syllable is the personal voice
of the psyche merging—*Yes*.
Knowing that a completed version
exists in the adjacent room,
I repeated—*Yes!*

Building up shadows
she stepped us through the second gate
in short lyrics and numinous moving images
recited by the descenders, each incarnated moment
preserved through their ascent.

Visions of cat claws and steely knives
large flies with purple gleaming bodies
flying owls along deep valleys.
There was a smell of autumn in the air
and of coal smoke, from a passing train.

IV. Dreams & Paradoila

Through fitful sleep and fever
the gypsy's admonition
played upon Oksana's mind:
> *It is not needful for thee to see with thine eyes*
> *the things that are in secret!* [1]

Perhaps in her sleep, I'll be entwined
I don't know if I'm awake, or living out a dream
I can neither laugh nor cry.
> *And then a dream, a dream amazing*
> *came into my slumbers.* [2]

Again the potholes, preserved for decades
emanating the close, foul breath
of human beings, rising
ceaselessly to the surface
accompanied by the muffled rumble of a train.

Forever leading to the Sanatorium
enamel spittoons, blood-flecked phlegm,
rushes of blood to the head, fainting spells,
insomnia and overpowering sexual urges,
changing color and texture of skin.

Amidst the walls, spotted with stains
candlelit shadows cast a pale face, drawn and tired
wearing a black broad-brimmed hat, guarding
melancholy, wondering eyes
suddenly withdrawing, like the phases of the moon.

Three Poets circle a burning manuscript, chanting:
> *Oh bury me, then rise ye up*
> *and break your heavy chains*
> *and water with the tyrant's blood*
> *the freedom you have gained.* [3]

Out of the fire, a talking cat
hands me 75,000 minuscule words
wedged onto fifteen sheets of vellum.
    Manuscripts never burn
    in the spirited chasms that yawn!

The sun sets, the mountains darken
as radical, revolutionary, romantic fade from view.
    Go where the owl flies
    along deep valleys,
    there you will find...

1. Apocrypha: Sirach Chapter 3
2. Taras Shevchenko, "The Dream"
3. Taras Shevchenko, "My Testament"

V. The Book of Remembrance

In the book of remembrance it is written:

In the city of Uman there was a Poet
whose thinking and brooding took him deep.

One Friday he stayed in the House of Study to think,
snared in his thoughts he tried to untangle
the question of the three hares.

A holy seer felt this from afar
and leapt to meet him,
reaching the House of Study
in only an instant.

There sat the Poet to which the seer replied:
you are brooding on whether IS is
and yet, a fool such as I
sees at a glance and believes!

To which the Poet's heart stirred
opening wide the Third Gate

unleashing the Tributaries of Poetic Fancy.

VI. The Third Gate

On the third day of the new moon
with Oksana well, we hiked the hill
behind Sataniv's Holy Trinity Monastery.
In the blackish distance, three portals loomed
abrupt and pointed steles stone.

In front of this Dark Gate
deceased grass and one thornless rose
form a lonely motif
where 300 carved gravestones bore witness
to the democracy of divine descent.

Desire heightened by the proximity of death
stepping lightly we glided, not knowing
how to navigate the forces at work
inside and outside, the palaces
where several sages lie.

Oksana recalled the Gypsy's vision
of mystics encircled by flames and lightning
journeying through multiple layered heavens
celestial realms guarded over by angels,
lions and golden griffins.

> *Beware the greedy eye*
> *that scans the world's edges*
> *to see if he can seize*
> *a land to bring unto the coffin.* 4

Alas, we found the Poet's gravestone
while ash trees creaked and creaked again
the riddle solved as lightning struck.
A carved illusion—a visual thkine
the Triskele of Three Hares!

Deep in earth's bosom,
beyond the veil of appearances
a chill, penetrating grief whispered,
    Rise free from ashes!
Emanating into harmony and order, illuminating
what we were really there for.

4. Taras Shevchenko, "Dream, A Comedy"

VII. Exit the Noumenon

Looking down the path
our backs turned to Sataniv, departing
in Bohmian trajectories.
Time a never-ending circle
mapping continual returnings and reflections.

Leaving behind a panoramic view
of windowless boxes, black earth and potholes
the library of Babel—noise
filled in a slice of time
by the turning of the bones.

Off to Kiev, №13 Andriyivsky's Descent.
As night falls on St. Vladimir's Hill,
we dine with Brothers Cyril and Methodius
who regale with the Dance of Polovtsian Maidens
and fading glories of Maidan.

A black cat keeps watch upon the gate
as the orange sun descends o'er Dnipro,
while three Poets mourn
   Regular meter, irregular rhyme
   a Cossack's shadow of the mind.

Pained over the memory
of the Night of the Murdered Poets
yet pleasured over the path to Parnassus,
she leaned her head upon me, muttering
   Twas lighter to be blind. [5]

Somewhere in space, I hang suspended
listening to the tamping machine
filling potholes with ballast of burnt clay.
Our last solitary coach passes endless squat houses
and a landscape the color of drizzle.

Far beyond the dark territory of the bellmouth
amidst every ravine that is my home—
the arts remain a minefield. Yet,
three Priestly Imprisoned Poets beckon me
to enter the Waker's Corridor.

5. Emily Dickenson, "From Blank to Blank"

15

AI

The Earth is degenerating these days. Bribery and corruption abound. Children no longer mind their parents, every man wants to write a book, and it is evident that the end of the world is fast approaching.

—Assyrian Stone Tablet, c.2800BC

Antic Interpretations

Casting ambiguous shadows
across the flanks of followers
looming before us in a blur of roles
eminent-looking psychologists
masquerade like circus animals
parading empty chairs.
Beached whales in submission
contemptuously blowing smoke
in tones of self pity.
Utopian dreamers
in angry marches, while
expanding horizons
of war and oppression
rewrite history—
like post cards
their colors faded and garish.

Arcane Infallibility

The Eagle Forum
born to discipline and punish
hurries to spread the Word.
Quivering—they hope to flourish
producing slavish followers
with brutish interpretations of ancient history
trapped in a world of neurotic corruption
a prison walled with hate.
Adorned in purple—they discover
Casper Milquetoast parading
proud antenna tops the trinity
priestly robes once worn in earnest
now stained in scarlet
from Liberty's whipping post.
Hearts turned to stone
as hymnals repeat the mantra:
    Like slaves and soldiers, ask no questions.

We are all insects. Groping towards something terrible or divine.

—Philip K. Dick, *The Man in the High Castle*

Anno Inventionis

Scientists with sleight of hand
present themselves as unimpeachable
while eschewing grandly global theories
penetrating the secrets
of a world beyond their understanding
they dare apostasy.
Into the age of information
we fill the void
remoteness from our own lives
all lost in sartrean existentialism
unable to escape
the malaise of our own history.
Fidelity to a simulacrum
can never restore
our lost innocence.

The child is the best philosopher.

—Wordsworth

Appreciative Inquiry

Politicians living lives
in narrowing circles
gaze no further
than the stoop where questions remain
unresolved in their hearts.
Books sealed in rooms
penned by foreign tongues
foretell distant days.
Shorn of answers
partisans stall, believing
the past was not predictable when it started.
Gone the magenta worldview—
now capital punishment
is our way of demonstrating
the sanctity of life!

It doesn't take many words to speak the truth.
—Hinmatóowyalahtqit

Lorem Ipsum

Revisionists content to lie
amidst the innocence of antiquity
turn their backs on truth
instead of pressing forward in pursuit.
Thinned by ignorance
they take pride in walking backwards
covering father's nakedness—
Ham's unpardonable offense
foretelling endless polemics
of the victor's ambitious son.
Glossing over Maoist purges
in the land of promise, we find
beneath a quaint facade
the island hides many thousands
gone through the door of no return
toward a home that bleeds
open wounds of history
slicing sacred sites, with

banal property lines.

Gnatola ma no kpon sia, eyenabe adelan to kpo mi sena.
(Until the lion has his or her own storyteller,
the hunter will always have the best part of the story.)
—Ewe-mina Proverb

Fantastic Servant, Horrible Master

One-dimensional man
—kalashnikovs of tomorrow
burn villages to hinder the advance of the Duke
select and engage targets
without human intervention
ubiquitous and cheap
kollateralschaden
abstract, agentless, and affectless
like friendly fire.
Aesopian language
where critical thought withers away
passing beyond the uncanny valley
into the plains of hyper-reality
insulated from any feelings
of repulsion and outrage
left only with the chimera of freedom
for the sake of those
declining in morale and hope.

سرگردان مسافر

The traveller has to knock at every alien door to come to his own, and one has to wander through all the outer worlds to reach the innermost shrine at the end.

—Rabindranath Tagore, *Song XII, Gitanjali*

Ad Infinitum

AI wandering
in the end, searching
through every alien door
a wilderness of worlds
missing the elusive art
of human functioning
remembering, repeating, reworking
bereft murmurs and ripples
accompanying the stream of life
an urge, a sigh, a dream
the tension of possibilities
staring or looking away
drifting away in a vague cliché.
For can one AI love another–
believe in forms, tones, words
or embrace brokenness
as an integral part of life?
That is perhaps the most difficult of all—
this is the heart of the matter.

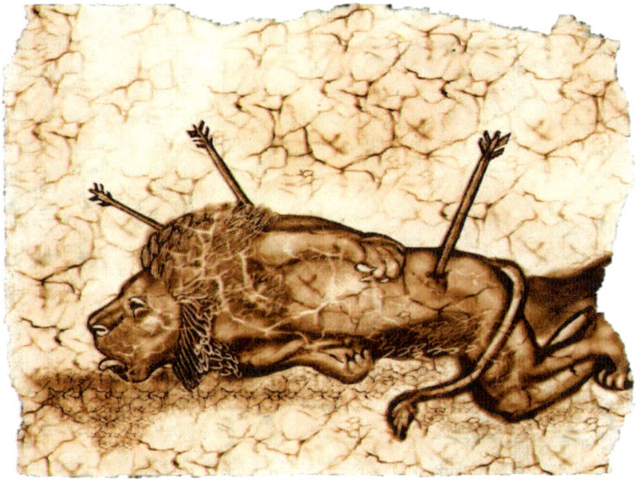

AI

Amen

Other Memories

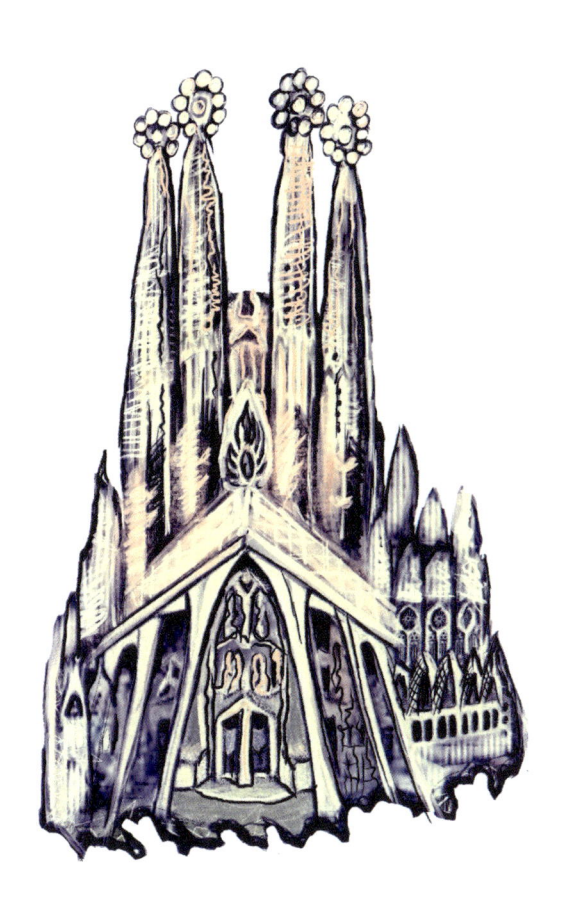

Song to a Dying Post

A Dying Post
rested in the swell
straight–and punctual
oblivious to the motion

Thou cross wind
became thy foe
to stand against
in stiff defiance and defense

As t'wer a blow
to thy tender base
while the waters ebbed and flowed

Sublimated in thy watery grave
the Dying Post
yielded nay to soft decay

Planted deep within
the harbors earthly skin
through gravel, grit, and soil
thy auger bore

You staked your case
an argument against
the laws of nature
you have no use for

No room for error in your stance
stand straight—Dying Post
do not bend or bow to any wind

Witness to estrangement
the isolated life
exalted and alone

Before thy base dost break
all protocol observed
eulogize a Dying Post
redemption song unearthed.

Extracting Gold

Extracting Gold
to halt the Exodus
of migrants and refugees.
Extracting Gold
to build a wall
around the Schengen free.
Extracting Gold
one vote cast
smells like blood and smoke.
Extracting Gold
to pay for razor wire
down in Jodenbreestrat.
Extracting Gold
to pay the price for something
they received for free.
Extracting Gold
to pay the right for blood drawn
stealing color from their cheeks.
Extracting Gold
short-term memory—shoes and coats
baby dolls piled high in Krakows Ghetto.
Extracting Gold
symbolic yes
like this star blazing on my arm.
Extracting Gold
romanticized internment camps
cold February forty-two.

Extracting Gold
this poem's goosestep, watching
neighbors marching to the precipice.
Extracting Gold
to maintain
a thin veneer of prosperity.
Extracting Gold
ten thousand silent footsteps
from Damsacus to St. Paul
echoing in parliament—
a caution to us all.
Extracting Gold
for Judas to repay
interest on the silver
long rotting in decay.

On The Road with Jack Kerouac

Long ago, they snapped fingers
to the beat of Jack Kerouac
and 6 poets at 6 gallery
with their goatees, berets, and bongos.
Like a guilty pleasure
they'd *Howl*
at the way Dick Shawn
did his groovy dance
in *It's a Mad Mad Mad Mad World*.
Far Out!

Last night, children laughed
at the self-conscious man
dancing to the trance-like rhythms
of the Sweet Pumpkin Marimba Band.
Only minor characters
at the City Lights Bookstore
out of context
like *A Cold Spring*
ah, the stupor and ecstasy of drugs.
Go! Go! Go!

Tonight, Pastor Ted improvises
walking on water
under City Lights,
a crazy dance
of crystal meth
and a *Naked Lunch*.
Abject people, down and out
and *The Lost Generation*
of Angry Young Men ask *How?*
It's a Mad Mad Mad Mad World!

Carnival Dream

Last night I watched the news
and thought of where we've gone wrong
makin' fun of people's difference
barring people from our homes

I sat at the doorstep
wonderin' how we'd changed
how did we all get here
how did the world turn so strange

I spent a year in Pristina
loved the people and their ways
especially how they looked upon
the star spangled flags that waved

Once it stood for something
perhaps a land that seemed to know
what we all would stand for
and things that we just won't

Tears flowed as I watched him
mock a better man
a carnival barker magnifying
the inaudible whispers of our souls

Tonight we sit wonderin'
how it's all changed
and can we ever get back to
a world with a little grace

The Making of a Myth

Ye old man wobbled down the Vinnytsian road
Hazel the goat straggling lazily by his side
Seeing an oil painting tucked under her arm
He called out for a look-see
He had been an artist once
Long ago in Paris ... or was it New York?
He spoke a little English ... or was it French?
Who could have guessed
That out there on the Bug *(pronounced Boog)* River
An English-speaking, French artist,
Ukrainian goat herder
Would break the silence
Erected by two thousand miles
A voice shouting from the mountainside
In a foreign tongue.
Many years later, I would think of him
One morning, skirting puddles
His name now faded from memory
One too many mornings and
Two thousand miles behind *(thanks Robert)*
But not Hazel
      I still remember her name!
She appears to me quite often
As a horned goat made of bronze and dressed in gold
Adorning a coat of arms flying high above the fields
Where Albanian goat herders dream of 1912
When narratives of innocence were established.

Surf's Faint Roar

The edge of the world
descends towards a sheltered shore.
Seaweed and tide pools
separated by a pebbly strand,
blocked by driftwood
and fallen pines intertwined.
We thread a path through
this passage puzzle.

Looking for sheltered faces,
we scramble through narrow passageways.
Petroglyphs anchor the foreland
narratives battered by the sea,
carvings of people who knelt before
a wedding, a child is born, a death—
t'siq'ati, t'siq'ati, t'siq'ati
lifeways written in stone.

Kayostla Beach at high tide
morning breaks at low.
Seastacks jutting close to shore
and seagulls rise to greet us—
sentinels of the coast.
We set out to the rhythm of the waves,
swinging wide around the headland
ascending up and inland.

Hemlocks dense and dewy canopies
open into Ahlstroms Meadow—
always something blooming.
Keep your eyes wide
and glean your reflection
cast from the boardwalk bridge
arching through the soggy fen.
Our faces, shimmering nearly one and the same.

With heavy hearts, our blissful stay
at Cape Alava neared its end.
As high winds whipped ocean spray
over silent reefs, we struck our tents.
Promising ourselves we would return
our hearts too breached to say,
that this would be another memory
bleached to pale gray.

Sparkling Eyes Zwedru

Sparkling eyes Zwedru
from the other side
little hands reach inward
towards affluence reaching out

Sparkling eyes Zwedru
extending peace and gratitude
from the other side
through a bitter kola nut

Sparkling eyes Zwedru
I never felt poverty
till I touched your tiny hand
on the other side

Sparkling eyes Zwedru
signs of peace
on the road to nowhere
on the other side

Where a bitter kola nut
feeds a sweet illusion
that poverty, hunger, corruption
are a million miles away

The Quiet One

Mom never understood why he didn't talk more. She insisted—he retreated to the workshop where the bandsaw shouted down the chatter. Dad died at fifty-three in seventy-nine. No calling to say farewell. No card either. He was quiet that way.

Forever

Aunt Marge took charge. She was strong that way. As if well-meaning clamor could wake the dead.

After the main event, cacophony dissipated. Seeking refuge back in halls of reputation, surrounded by the noble few, thunderous silence enveloped the quiet one.

Forever

Sister Shelley told everyone—*don't bother him. If he needs you —he'll let you know.* But he never did. He was quiet that way. She misunderstood.

Many years later, tragedy struck too soon. On a loud garish unforgiving slope, coming home. Gone at twenty-one in fifteen.

Forever

Facebook renders *Dies irae, dies illa*. No room for quiet there. I reached out to my old friend. Not hard to do. Really. Lots of water and no real bridge to speak of.

But time has a way of angling back around to where ephemerality reminds us of the necessity to reach out with tender spirit voices.

Whatever your nature, make sure you penetrate the wall of sound by speaking in the knowing that it's not your voice that matters.

Forever

Sagrada Familia

Semiotic scaffolding began before I could speak
mother and father provided a joint picture book
bedtime prayers and read alouds

Architects adept at building scaffolds
they adjusted the transoms to fit the occasion
over the course of many seasons

Out of the straight lines and crooked timber
textured complexes anchored
undergirding my shadow self

In recent years I've had a recurring dream
in which I am perpetually trapped
in the Basilica of the Sagrada Familia

Peering out through vaulted stained glass windows
I glimpse blank faces on the streets below
they cannot see me for the scaffolds

Fronting facades cast dark angular shadows
guarding tormented characters
along the suffering way

I canvass naves, vaults, and inner accommodations
anxiously looking for an exit—or a temple
where solitude will overcome my isolation

Internal scaffolding creates many specters
that block expansion, interrupt all joy
impede paths to the expiatory temple

One gaunt wraith hits my blind side
illuminating an invisible saurian tail
dragging behind like some monster nigh

Only at night, when no shadows exist
can I pass through intuition's borders
where my companion no longer glowers

Under lacarnes' illuminating light, I stand between mirrors
one face forward, one looks back—I see
the temple's entrance via different corridors

My soul in the throes of melancholy
I enter the temple through a catenary arch
where surrounding forest awakens my drowsy heart

In dizzying verticality, bone-like columns twist and bend
like cypress branches reaching upward in resolution
toward the canopy of heaven

Bathed in azure beams of unity—my truest friend
all cavils running around my head upend—in triumph
I see myself as streamlets flow
the way I truly am.

The Last Word

In the end
Michael fell
From the word
That did dwell
Behind a wall
Beneath a well
Of pain and hurt
A comic's knell
What lingered there
No one could quell
The sounds we heard
A dim bombshell
How oft the word
Leaves such a smell
That we should run
From there pell-mell
And curse the day
The ne'er-do-well
Leapt straight into
His private hell
Parting sadly
With no farewell
He takes his leave
For the jester's bridewell

c. 2006

Coda: A Paean for Peter Francis Wilmot
circa 1978
Overlooking Bellingham Bay

Worms

Made in the USA
Lexington, KY
28 December 2016